"This book started out as a compelling story about Serena's life. We followed her from childhood to where she is today. We read about her struggles. We saw how she worked to make her dreams become reality. Half way through the book started an enlightening education on how to take the blame away from others and turn it back to ourselves. We learned to focus. This is an amazing book that has been written to help Serena document her story and her methods – and to help the reader save energy by using her techniques.

Fay Gabrielson

"As I read your story, I hope you will forgive that I did not feel sorry for you (I believe that was your intention). Your story is told in such a matter of fact way, it does not dwell on the details of your circumstances, it just demonstrates that there were barriers that you have overcome with courage, resilience, heart and challenges each of us to "Get out of our own way". I must admit my heart broke for the child but beamed for the woman.
Your story and your process to overcome barriers in your life should be read by everyone and I hope that millions of people connect with you, to have you help them be their best self. "

Linda Prafke

"Riveting. Enjoyable and I admire the authenticity and raw communicative writing."

Kimberly Jolivet

HOW I GOT OUT OF MY OWN WAY "MY JOURNEY FROM HOPELESS TO HAPPYNESS"

You can redefine your past, present & future.

You deserve the best!

HOW I GOT OUT OF MY OWN WAY
MY JOURNEY FROM HOPELESS TO HAPPYNESS
©2017 **SERENA DALLAS**. ALL RIGHTS
RESERVED

ISBN: 978-0-9959825-0-5 book

To my amazing children Amanda & Kyle,
my partner in life; Blair & to the
abundance of people who have supported
me throughout the years.
In good times & in bad each of you has
shown me the way to be responsible for
my life and to be engaged in it.

Thank you for all your loving support!

TABLE OF CONTENTS

Introduction

A LITTLE GABBING

BEFORE WE START

This book is dedicated to a special group of individuals who have seen me through the good, the bad and at times, the very unpleasant parts of my life.

First, to my children Amanda and Kyle; two of the greatest gifts ever bestowed upon me; who to this day still love me in my imperfectness. Kids (yes, I know you are full grown adults, but you are always my kids) I cannot express how blessed I am. How I thank the universe every day that I am here to see how each of you grew up to be powerful and beautiful adults. You both have a tremendous amount of compassion in your hearts; the best part for me as a parent is to see that you are freely giving it back to the world. Your very presence in my life reminds me of all that is great and wonderful in the world. Thank you for staying in my life; through all the hurts and the sorrows, and showing and extending forgiveness even when it has taken me years to accept it. Of course, for being part of all the GREAT in my life as well.

Thank you also to my bestie – Rosanne. Yes, I realized that this is incorrect terminology; I really don't care. This courageous woman has stood beside me in my darkest hours. Stood beside me even when I was cruel and hurtful. Even during her own trials and tribulations she always took the time to encourage me in ways that truly shows Gods forgiving grace and what it means to be freely loved. During my very darkest of days, she prayed, visited and even when I turned her away, she remained steadfast in "being there".

This story could not even have been started without my mother. She has provided everything she could to bring about the woman who is here today. I also acknowledge, she chose to give birth to a child even though her life was not easy. There could have been many options for her, yet she did the most courageous. Thank you, mom. Yes, we share differences; it never changes the fact that I love you more than anything. You were and are still a good mother. I love and respect you with all that I am.

I am fortunate to have grown up with my older (yes, I had to get that in!) brother and two younger sisters. While it is true, we are all no longer close to each other like we were when we were younger; and yes, this does create deep sorrow for me. I also know that each of us carries a story and a journey. While I tell this story of my journey thus far; it is all based on my personal experiences and my perspective. I am quite sure each of us could write a book or two about our journeys. I certainly am not perfect and have made a *vast* number of mistakes.

When they read this version of my life, I hope each of you sees that I don't blame the past or any person for hardships that I faced. Instead, I value each you individually and collectively as you have shaped my life, taught me valuable life lessons and even have reminded me that I need to honor where I have come from.

I also need to say a dear "thank you" to a variety of organizations. Such as the Peter Lougheed Hospital for the mental health services and support that I received for almost three years. This critical step is another reason why I advocate on behalf of having discussions about mental health often; not just one or two days a year. The stigma needs to be broken down in a real and meaningful way. Another organization is Dress for Success. This incredible not-for-profit organization came to me as a referral 13 years ago. Without their support, I would not have entered the workforce with the opportunity to land gainful employment with the right clothing. They provided the extra external confidence that helped change my life. For this reason, I continue to volunteer and be an ambassador for them even to this day!

I want to also acknowledge my life partner Blair. He has truly shown me what unconditional love is. He has supported me over the past few years in a variety of ways. Without a doubt, he has been crucial in helping me accept that it's okay "not being perfect". It amazes me that he has been the first male person to ride the emotional roller coaster with me instead of on the sidelines. Because of his own. fierceness for life, he encouraged me to finish this book. Even providing sound feedback in my life along supporting me in meaningful ways. I admire, respect and love him dearly.

Finally, I need to express a heartfelt "thank you" to you the reader. You are the one taking the time to pick up this book. It will be frankly the most honest, raw and at times vulnerable book you will read from a person who really thought they were an open book ~ yet I wasn't. This book will be strewn with facts and realities that will hopefully inspire you to reach out and understand how trauma from an early age can dramatically affect a life negatively; and how it can also help shape a life of strength. The irony of my journey is that while I suffered at the hands of the very people I cared & trusted the most; the flip side is that I learned my courage and strength came amid it. I believe there is a beauty to be seen, even from tragedy.

I learned you don't have to be defined by your past. You don't even have to allow it to rule your life. I have since learned that I can take responsibility without it crushing me any longer. I can accept the abuse without the hurt or shame. I can even accept that there are days where I fall into a "victim mentality" but no longer reside there as my safety net. I do not "blame" anyone anymore. The onus is on me to create my life. Not hold it hostage to the past. Especially the past that may be distorted.

I have learned to embrace my humanness. At the same time, I cringe at the thought that for some reason I actually thought I was a defective person. A person who "should have never been born" because I seemed to attract all the wrong things in my life. I cringe when I think about the hurt I caused my children whom I love more than any being on this planet (the past or present or future). I was a broken person who just couldn't see the light of beauty that was; just me. I sometimes cringe at all the wasted time and then I am reminded. I then become filled with joy because I still have all this time to be the person that I was meant to be. As longs as I choose to!

This question used to come to me at different times of my life, ***"Did you know you have time to be the person you choose to be?"*** It would dumbfound me as I would wonder what was the point. My hope is you read the journey that I have been on, from Hopeless to Happyness; you will "see" the point. Hopefully, you too will learn some lessons along the way – with the goal of it being easier to learn than I did.

As you read this book; think often of the challenges you face. They need not compare to mine. In fact, my hope is that yours is easier. Just don't let those challenges hold you back. Refuse them and don't let them define you; instead, let them inspire and motivate you to be more.

More real.

More vulnerable.

More gifted.

More joyous.

More filled with life.

My honest request, desire and challenge to you with all that is in me. Is that you to take in life and decide, this is your life.

Love it & Live it!

With much respect & admiration,

Serena

There must be a beginning....

WHAT DO YOU MEAN "HOW I GOT OUT OF MY OWN

WAY"? THE STORY OF THE TITLE

This journey starts with the title. So, that's where I shall start. With some background information and a simple explanation. The concept of a book came to me around 2004, yet it came with a completely different title. During this time, I had released a whopping 180 pounds of weight off of my body. Yes, I released the weight not lost it. This was something I had no intentions of ever finding again.

I also started mentoring others to live a healthier lifestyle. With that there were lots of questions asked; clearly about weight release; but then also about the story of my weight gain in the first place. It was because of these questions, people suggested that I write a book about "my powerful story". For years, I laughed at the very idea. Seriously, the lady who had horrible English and is scared to death of people; consciously writing a book. "Sure, I'll get right on that!" I used to say.

Then one day a title came to mind it was "Hey You get out of the way!" clear out of nowhere. It seemed like a great title and whenever I mentioned it to people, it resonated. Mainly because over time I realized "I WAS THE ONE IN MY OWN WAY. It made sense that my sub-conscious was telling me to "Hey You, Get Out of The Way". That title stuck in my head for years, from the very first time I thought of writing the journey of my life thus far. It stuck because, unbelievably, there was a time where I believed I was in complete control of everything and yes, even everyone.

Then I realized something.

Shit, it was my first

Reality Check

I, Serena Caprice Dallas, lived an utterly total lie.

Yep, this is when I realized that my life had several, what I now call *"**Reality Checks**"*. You're going to come across many of them in this book all written **"Reality Checks"** in bold. It's intentional. These are the defining moments in my life where I stood at the edge of a cliff in my life and I was faced with a reality. I had a choice to make. Every now and then one must be exceptionally real with themselves and it's usually not very pretty. For me, it was up until my early 30's. I was so critically out of touch with how I perceived the world.

As a matter of fact, when I experienced my first **"Reality Check"** - I was in complete denial. Remember, I actually "felt" and believed wholeheartedly that I controlled everything, yet the reality was I controlled nothing.

For F's sake, I had excuses for everything that happened in my life up to 2001. They all seemed completely valid too. It was so bloody effing' easy to have an excuse. Easy to get others to have pity for me. It was also too easy for me to not take any responsibility. Even though I felt I was the only responsible one in my circle.

Contradictions abounded in my life. I said aloud to everyone that I blamed no one, yet I lived my life "blaming" something, someone, some experience – well frig, anything. Truth be told the one person I forgot to "blame" or more accurately "hold accountable" was myself; Serena Caprice Dallas.

As in all stories or journeys, some order or context is needed in order to help bring understanding. To get a better sense of what I mean; I will share some real honest shit. I will tell you my life has been one hell of a ride. Full of ups, downs and slapped upside the head sideways. All I ask, is that you sit back, take off all preconceived judgments and join me on this journey where I went from Hopeless to Happyness.

Yes, Happyness with a Y. Years ago I read a book by Chris Gardner titled "The Pursuit of Happyness". It struck me as a book that is so similar yet completely different. Needless to say, it touched me deeply. It is stated that this is the American Dream. The pursuit of happiness is what Chris wanted for himself and his son. What I believe is everyone wants happiness in every area of their lives. The key to me was the "Y" in this story. What I took from it and how I use it in my story, HappYness. I chose to spell it this way intentionally. My life has become very intentional. I CREATE and DEFINE my life, my happiness. With that, I also take in all accountability for it. Happyness is a choice that can only happen when you have been intentional and accountable in creating it. I am happy and filled with happyness. even when my life is in rut, slump or has a bout of chaos. I am happy because I chose to be.

Now comes a forewarning, I have the worst grammar. My writing this journey is not meant to be perfectly written or even to follow the rules of writing. You will notice punctuations in the wrong places, nouns, verbs etc. not necessarily used in correct context. SCREW IT! I decided to write very much like I talk. With it, I also got rid of my excuses of why I couldn't write about the journey. I did this to inspire more of a conversation sort of like me being right there with you; sharing the story. I am by nature a storyteller as you will see. I sometimes go on a tangent, but I always come back to the point; *eventually*.

At the time of the finalizing of this writing, I am forty-seven years old. Remarkably, my journey of enlightenment is but a mere 16 years old. This year actually, I celebrate my sweet sixteen. I have come to understand that I am in control of only one thing. Nope, it's not "life" that I am in control of. The only thing I am in control of 100% is me. I am in complete control of my thoughts, actions, and even the consequences. Yes, I have complete control over only over that. Yet it is the most powerful control each of us has.

So, I mentioned how my life was built on a variety of excuses. Many of those excuses led to unfulfilled promises. Some of them were promises to my kids. I vividly remembering a promise to the kids that one day we as a family will go to Disneyland. Don't know when but somehow, we are going to get there. I even remember saying aloud once to myself "One day I'll have money and our kids will see just how much we love them simply because we went." I also had excuses like it was "someone else's fault" that we could not or rather, did not go. Like in some many things I had excuses, promises and "wishes". There is that great saying, hindsight is always 20/20. I tragically spent many years blaming others for the internal sufferings I had. Blaming my mother, my paternal father who, I felt, chose to not be in my life. I then moved on to blaming my stepfather, my brother, my sisters and to top it off, I even blamed my ex-husband.

*At the time, not once did the thought occur that **I** had*

*any **responsibility** at any given moment to be*

***accountable** for my life.*

This thought alone is what prompted me to write this journey/self-help book. I sincerely don't want you to waste valuable time like I did. Regardless if you are older or younger you can still see through my lessons that you DO HAVE POWER. You can choose to live a fulfilling life much sooner than I did.

I feel like there is a caveat here. There is shared responsibility here in various ways which you will discover. What I do want to focus on though is by my late 30's it was finally time to let go of excuses.

I hope you can see the point. That I was completely in my own way of my own life. I took no responsibility. It did seem natural to believe it was "because" of something else. When this working title "Hey You, Get Out of The Way: changed to "How I Got Out of My Own Way" it became real as far as the "how I chose to change *my* life". It required me to get out of my own way and I needed to start to take responsibility.

Reality Check

- ***Be serious***, *you cannot change the past. You cannot go back and make things "right".*

You can, however, grow from this moment on.

- **Pay attention** to see how much I lost out of my life, learn from some of my mistakes (oh dear lord, tell me I am not the only one who made them!) and from this moment on, choose to create the life you feel is living inside of you and making it your reality!

My one and only regret about this journey of mine is a simple *"Why did it take so long to finally understand this process?"*

I am choosing to not dwell on this fact because again, you cannot change a single iota in your life until you are willing to acknowledge that something needed to change.

You deciding to read my journey indicates to me that you also are interested in living a successful life. Successful on your own terms, just like I am doing now.

I am successful.

Am I rich?

Yes, in my soul.

Do I get the opportunity to share my story – hell yes!

This is a success to me.

Oh, by the way, life doesn't care how old you are; or for that matter how young you are. Right now, you are at the perfect time of your life to sincerely, learn how to get out of your own way. The coaching part of me says, "Take the time to learn tidbits from my journey." The reality is if I can save you years and years of holding back, help you to discover that fire burning in your gut of your authentic self and then to act on it. Then all of the shit I've gone through will have all been worth it.

Worth it because you will be adding additional light in this world that someone is just waiting for.

Worth it, because with the sharing of this book, I will have shared some very secret places of me and learned vulnerability in the process. I am no longer held in bondage to the past; even as broken as I was; as hurt, confused, and bewildered with my life. I eventually realized that I had to do the work that was needed and became the person I was meant to me.

The story is not over – not by a long shot! Hell, I am still very young! I am embracing this moment and I even see the beautiful moments of my past. I am so excited and on fire for my future!

Here's a gentle reminder. The only person in your way; is you.

Just as it was with me.

CREATED WITH PERFECTION

It was written in the Universe long before she showed up. She was DESTINED to be here. To be born a magnificent being who would change the world around her. As destiny, had predicted it happened in the summer of 1969, she came into this glorious world. The child born to a set of parents both who were young and drastically overwhelmed. A time in the world where rebellion was the norm, the parents were a mere 17 years' young at the time of the birthing of their second child. The first child was only 11 ½ months older. The creative story overheard was about how the mother believed the second pregnancy was going to be a boy just like her first. Thus, the plan to name the second child, Charles James.

At the birth; discovery was that she did not give birth to another son, quite the opposite. The panic had set, the parents needed to figure out a name and to have it mean something. The story unfolds in the hospital room. The television set is one; the show that is playing is called, "Bewitched". The parents stop to watch as a means of escaping the reality of another child. The main character Samantha and her sister Serena were having a lively conversation at the right moment when they looked up. At that moment, something about the name rang out in the room. From that moment on, the name was destined to be **"Serena"** meaning clear, tranquil, serene. Or as I like to think, the fun witch!

Now, admittedly, I have heard several variations of this story growing up. The one thing is, they all come down to the fact that

A: no one knew that I was to be a girl

B: A name was not chosen for a possibility of a girl being born

C: Finally, "Bewitched" the television show was on the television set.

In my very early years of life though, hearing stories recounted over the years, I would have to say, my birth was not a huge overwhelming welcoming. From early on, I heard countless times how both my older brother and I were "*accidents*". Admittedly, as a child, I had no clue what this meant. What I did know though is that this left a hole in me that I just couldn't explain. It honestly only finally became clear to me in my early 20's. That is when I realized that was a common term to use for an unplanned pregnancy. Not necessarily that we weren't wanted, just an accident. Regardless though, this did not minimize that "hole" feeling and the early indoctrination in my life that one must "***earn love***" because I wasn't wanted therefore I needed to validate my existence.

Ironically this is the concept my story & this book.

REALITY CHECK

....it was learning to love me.......

The strangeness I felt in my life with that hole I felt because I was an "accident". I also had this conflicting feeling inside of me. I also had this overbearing sense of hope. I have no idea where it came from or really when I noticed it. All I know is from as early as I can remember, I always felt there was something I was destined to be or do. There was some sort of greatness to be achieved; something I was to give back to this world whom I felt had left me as an "accident". I had no clue or an idea of what that was to be. Ultimately though, by writing this book, I have a strong sense of the purpose as it stands now, but nowhere near to the full extent.

What I do know is that I will affect the world around me by the effect of my words. My journey into Happyness is a reminder to me & you. We can get our shit together. Regardless of what seemed like an "accidental" birth or even uneventful welcoming into the world.

Happyness is our
destiny and purpose!

I daydreamed a lot as a child which I guess all kids do. This in itself is not a "big whoop" and as such, this was never out of the ordinary. Here's the thing, as a child the fun part to me was that I would literally create stories in my mind and in my life to make it seem so much more. More alive, freer, just more of everything. I never had more possessions though, it was all about these "experiences".

Ultimately these stories became my lifeline to accepting my life as it was. I vividly remember several times I insisted to my mother and family members, I must be adopted since I felt that I had no connection whatsoever to my family. As an adult and mother, myself, I imagine now, how much this must have hurt my mother. Listen, I wasn't perfect either! But, I told myself this story over and over again and in my mind, it was real. As real as the air, I breathed each and every day.

One time, I even remember going to the extent of having a conversation with my Aunt to adopt *"me back"* so that I could live with her.

Even back then I was needing that

REALITY CHECK....

Other times though, I actually feared that I had lost all reality. Mainly because I had told myself such grand stories. The stories served two purposes. The stories kept me alive with my imagination going wild, but they also fragmented me because I believed far too intensely in them.

I do believe that life was kind enough to give me an amazing older brother. He and I were very close during the early stages of life. Being only about 11 months apart in age, meant we had each other to depend on. Now, don't get me wrong, we fought like most all siblings do and yes, he won many of those battles. My brother provided my first exposure to someone standing up for me. When I started school my "big brother" would willingly stand up protect me from anyone who would try to hurt me. You see, I was that child who didn't quite fit in with most. Me, the story teller, wild imagination and inability to connect with other. This made me a target for bullying with name calling and mocking. My brother though, me and him we would create some of the craziest games to play to amuse ourselves. Funny thing is it was normal for one of us get hurt in some way, but never seriously hurt. We always found a way to laugh amid our poverty that we were both born into.

My amazing brother, he has a tender heart that was scarred as we grew up. After the birth of my second child and my moving away to another province, we drifted apart for many years. But I also know that even though, each of us living our own lives; if I need him; he is here.

I am quite certain he doesn't understand that in those early days he was my first role model for a man. I am thankful he was and still is, the most protective person in my life. My brother was and forever will be my Superman. For years, it was him & I against the world. We were determined to win; although we had no clue what that meant.

Without my mother, there, of course, would be no me. There was a time when she was such a lively person. I remember as a small child.... she laughed so much; even though we didn't have much in the ways of material possessions, she did her best to raise two young children on her own after our paternal father decided he no longer wanted to remain in our lives. I say this with humility and understanding that there are two sides to every story. I as a parent of two children, I would move heaven & hell to see them. No one would ever stand in my way. Yes, I felt hurt that he would not come visit us.

REALITY CHECK....

This was my father's decision, no one else's. The unfortunate thing though, he has passed on. Regretfully, I will never have that chance to have a genuine father/daughter relationship.

Now, up until the age of five or six, I remember laughing a lot even though we had virtually nothing. I wanted my mom to love me fully. So, both me and my amazing brother we did our best and tried really hard to listen and behave properly. The irony is looking back as an adult. I have to admire her; my mom. She clearly had two very rambunctious children. One with a wild imagination and one with a protector nature. She did an incredible job with the very limited resources she had.

What I remember of my mom before my step-dad is that she was always "there". While I had this hole in my heart, I also saw how she laughed. We had nothing for possessions and yes we wanted more. Yet, how mom's laughter always gave me a sense of feeling loved. Actually, it was only when she laughed did I "feel" a sense of being loved. Hearing her laugh & smile meant everything to me.

Remember how I was saying that I felt like I was meant for big things? All during this time, it was still there, inside of me, this feeling of me being bigger than life. Me being on a stage; sharing with the world this message "Things can be grand! Life can be amazing and everyone can be happy!" THAT is what my mom's laughter did for me.

I just had no idea how to communicate or even explore that feeling. What I did know is that it never went away. Admittedly, it did get forgotten or shall I say misplaced, but it never went away.

As the song by Blue Suede goes, "*I'm hooked on a feeling, high on believing. That you're in love with me*". I knew, just knew, there was something out there for me.

There is another side to my mother whom I love with all of who I am. I freely acknowledge that, yes, she did her best. But as I got older though, that best fell short.

This brings me to a new chapter that was about to happen in our lives. It started when mom found a new love when I was about five or so years old. This new man seemed to be the perfect dad that both my brother and I were looking for and the man of her dreams.

That chapter though, about five years later would prove to be the start of my BLAME GAME. Also, when my life was to be changed forever and it would set me on a path of destruction.

Remember though:

I was a child born with a destiny

Just like you.

My early years were formed with some heartache but overall with a sense that life can be great even when we didn't have material possessions to show for it. By the time I was five, I had learned that love can be awesome. My mind processed it as, "get someone to laugh and see that smile that happens with the squinting of the eyes." But it does come with a cost – it must be earned.

Things have a way of working out and life can BE better; or so what I believed.

Until....

*"You will never understand the **hell***

I felt inside my head"

Unknown

Nope – Not Me, The Realization my Life is Set.

"I WOULD DO ANYTHING FOR LOVE…."

MEATLOAF

The addition of a new father into my life meant I had a new male role model to look up to. I was never so thrilled in my entire short life! my Dad (I never called him a step dad) was a charismatic and impactful person. He played with us, took us out and we did things together. But there was something; something lurking in the dark.

One of the first changes I noticed was that he drank a lot. I guess my mom did too, but it wasn't so pronounced like his drinking. Many times, the two of them were ok. I mean, they were fun there was singing and dancing in the house. It was like a party at times when they drank. Then there were those times when the big dramatic fights would happen. There was never the "small" disagreement; it was always holy hell. The yelling, fighting, the throwing of stuff. I was scared out of my mind. Not just for me but for all of us. Even then, my brother protected me as much as he could.

I sometimes would make the situation worse without knowing it by yelling at both of them to stop. Somehow though, my protector would end up taking a beating for me for the way I behaved. What I tried to prevent, to stop was the violence.

REALITY CHECK....

I could stop nothing.

I could do nothing.

I failed.

I would be crushed because I never wanted anyone to get hurt. I just couldn't stand the yelling, the shouting, and even more so, the throwing of stuff. Everything together made me a mess of nerves, a frightened child with nowhere to turn except to the stories. The stories I told myself got grander than ever before. My life was "perfect". I hid the bruises. Those bruises came in the form of emotionally, physically and mentally from everyone. Whenever I mustered the courage and tried to say something to someone; it couldn't be believed (in part to my storytelling & in part to him being so charismatic).

I lived in my emotional pain. It made me sad that I couldn't figure out why I couldn't seem to make my parents love us and to have him stop hurting us.

I talk clearly about me, but it wasn't just me, both my brother and I suffered. Looking back now, I understand that as children, we could not be expected to fix anything. It didn't stop us though. We couldn't seem to figure out the right way to behave to make sure the fights wouldn't happen. As always to violence, there was no rhyme or reason as to when it would start. It may have started with the drinking, but then it morphed to virtually anytime

I guess the biggest impact to me that started my journey of hopelessness was the punishments. Those punishments always without exception came from him. He was exceptionally cruel in his delivery. Any means that was readily handy he would use and those punishments mostly came from when he was drinking.

It seemed to me that my mom was powerless to step in and stop those punishments. Like I said before, there also seemed to be no rhyme or reason as to what would set it off. I can only really think of a few times where I, in reality, deserved punishments but **never ever** to the degree that I received them. Especially not with the violence.

I will say though, hidden amongst those alcoholically induced tirades, there were good memories too. They are harder to remember as clearly, the chaos overshadowed them.

Then one day, it all changed.

Isn't strange how you can look back and clearly remember a memory or emotion? For me, I remember that it was a sunny day. For years we had an established pattern of moving about every 6-8 months. At this time, we were living in the country – well ok, let's be real here. It wasn't so much country as opposed to the remote. We were not living "in the city" heck, there were only 3 houses within reach of each other. At least that is what my memory remembers. I knew something was changing in the house as there were plans to move from being out in the country to back into the city. Like I said, we moved around a lot but when we moved to the country. Basically, it was to get away from people. Hindsight, it was easier to have those physical outbursts and have fewer people know about them.

The BIG announcement came.

"Wants a little brother or sister?".

I was 9 or 10 at the time. I was beyond thrilled with this revelation. How could I not be, I was going to be a "**big sister**". The feeling was not as welcomed by my brother on the other hand. I even remember him stating the fact that it *"better be a boy; or else."* The things we say as pre-teens! I mean, I am not sure what his *"or else"* was in relation to, but I couldn't have cared less!

I was getting a real live BABY ALIVE DOLL!

Hey, those were the cat's meow back in the day. The opportunity though to have a real live baby that I can take care of. It was like a dream come true.

Little did I know....

It was during mom's pregnancy that my life as I knew it changed forever. When I didn't think that the physical & emotional abuse couldn't be outdone. That is when I learned the lesson in life.... people you love can be crueler than you can ever imagine.

The consistent sexual abuse came into my life. Beforehand it was random and "not done to me"

I knew it was wrong. I hated it. My whole being dealt with it as me being the bad girl who deserved the feelings of emptiness. Yes, of course, I was convinced that it was because I was loved me and I loved him. The justification used was that since I wasn't really his biological child, we were more like boyfriend and girlfriend.

I knew it was wrong, yet it still went on. I felt powerless and conditioned to not do anything or say anything for fear of further retribution. Who would believe me anyways? Everyone outside of the home felt he was this perfect person. I don't think anyone understood what really went on behind closed doors.

This part is without a doubt one of the hardest parts of my journey. It is relevant and yet irrelevant all at the same time. It was *THE* turning point. It turned my earlier life of hope, dreams and believing I was meant for more; to slow decaying of my emotional self; I was dying.

The self-hatred, loathing, and disdain that started to permeate my soul. The confusion of loving someone so much and hating them all at the same time. The actual cementing of earlier notions that love is earned & you better do whatever you can in order to get it. Because in reality – you don't deserve it. You don't deserve love or even life for that matter.

More on this later ----- maybe.

Anyways, back to my earlier recounting of my mom. She did go into labour early. Of course, the excitement and anticipation was all over the place. Even me, who had built the "new me" in order to deal with my new abusive realities. Admittedly, I was worried for my mom, since I had understood that mom had not gone to the end of her pregnancy and that this was not a good thing. I waited with anticipation for the news about my new brother or sister and if mom was ok.

He finally came home and what came out of his mouth was a pure shock.

"Ok guys; mom had the babies. You have sisters."

WAIT...HUH...WHAT?

The instant reaction to the word SISTERS was immediate. I felt like someone said something wrong.

Sisters?

The questions ran through my mind so fast. Does that mean there is more than one? How can that be? I had to ask.

"How did mom have more than one baby?"

TWINS

Have you ever known a word, yet have no clue what it really meant until one day a light bulb suddenly went on?

That is *exactly* how I felt that particular day.

There you go. One plus one equals two. TWINS.

EEKK, I am a big sister to two sisters.

How life was grand or so I thought.

The Grand Life

More than I Bargained For

Yes, I had to admit it. The grand life was short lived. Once they came home from the hospital they shared my room. At first, this was seriously everything one could ever hope for. I was caring for these beautiful babies. They shared one crib and remarkably even though they would be separated in that very large crib, they always found a way to be close to each other.

I also experienced another side. I was not prepared for parenting. The amount of work that goes into caring, diapering, feeding and trying to get sleep. I became "mom #2". The pregnancy, delivery and the realization of twins was without a doubt exceptionally hard on my mom. I don't say this as I know; just what I have learned. Because back in *those days*, no one ever talked about or even mentioned postpartum depression like we do now. In this day and age, we recognize it better and understand the effects that pregnancy & delivery can have on a woman.

Unfortunately, though, for my mom, she unknowingly suffered dramatically and my dad had no clue what to do or even how to help. He became more of a drinker (which seemed impossible) and she more withdrawn. Both of them though, now incapable of taking care of four children.

This experience alone formed my new philosophy on life. A place where fathers had sexual relationships with daughters; learning how to parent and take care of children, I vowed just after my 12th birthday, I would never have children. How could I? I never ever wanted to expose a child to the extent of abuse I had suffered and continued to suffer until I was 16. If I wasn't good enough as I was, clearly, I was never good enough to be a mother and actually be a good parent in general. This was just too much work.

Please don't get me wrong, I desperately loved my sisters beyond measure. I mean, they looked at me with such pure unconditional love; something I felt I'd been missing in my life up to that point. But damn it, it was hard work. Going to school and keep my grades up even though I would be worried about the girls until I got home. Then I'd fall into "mom mode" until bed. I was exhausted all the time.

The abuse did not stop either. Actually, it became more prevalent. Depression and both parents' inability to cope meant more drinking was happening in the home. Virtually daily and the outbursts were erratically random.

As crazy as my life seemed, I knew that I would end up creating the same life that my mother made. So, I made this vow for myself.

I would work hard in school; as hard as I could. I would not accept poverty as my reality and more importantly, I would never *ever* depend on anyone.

I would work my ass off and I would get my high school diploma. Then carry on to post-secondary education and make a real life for me. The life as some amazing business professional and I would oversee a group of people who would listen and respect me. I would teach and empower them how to get things done quickly and efficiently while still talking nicely to people; not mean or hurtful.

I would make a $75,000 a year, have my own home, car with a credit card. It would have to be an American Express card because only the wealthy and respected people had an American Express credit card. Oh, how grand of a story I told myself. I *made* myself believe this.

Just before my 16th birthday, I realized I had my first....

Reality Check

- I lived in poverty.

- UP until this time we moved what seemed like every 6 to 8 months. I had gone to 2 high schools and about 10 primary schools.

- Love was not shared freely; it always came with a cost.

- Our family was racked by substance abuse, alcohol abuse, physical, emotional, mental & financial abuse. No one in the family was immune to this. As sure as the air I breathed, I considered my life was now set and it was in essence, over.

Apparently, it didn't matter what I wanted. By all accounts, it seemed that this was what I had to look forward too for the rest of my life.

The Middle Part

"I AM A SIMPLE PERSON WHO HIDES A THOUSAND
FEELINGS BEHIND THE HAPPIEST SMILE"

Oh, the irony because I write this that there was a bright side. Remember when I said as a young child I felt like I was destined for "something". Well, it was combined with another trait that has never left me. The uncanny ability to see something good amongst all the darkness. To see the positive in a negative.

Anyways, my mom was always on my case to get good grades. I could never understand why she kept pushing me so hard. I mean it seemed anything less than an 80% meant lectures upon lectures of why I didn't try harder.

Both parents used what they considered "well-meaning phrases" were received and interpreted differently.

Phrases such as... "You're smarter than this why are you being so stupid." This one specifically stood out to me as it broke me each time I heard it. Even to this day, I cringe and it breaks my heart when I hear anyone call anyone 'stupid' or use other demeaning names to "emphasize" a point. This phrase that I heard over and over again was the slap in the face and what I call a backhanded compliment.

Ok, wait a second I have a soap box right here. Here is a short PSA. Everyone is exceptionally capable of great things. This is what we as a society should be focusing on instead of the name calling. In all my years, I have never seen a person excel when torn down. Determined, maybe – but definitely not excel.

Okay, I got that out of my system. I am off the soap box and on with my journey.

My mothers' unwelcomed badgering about my grades meant that I did eventually receive my high school diploma. Despite all the shenanigans in my life, self-destructive behaviors that come from abuse. I will say that this is an achievement that I am still very proud of today. In case you wonder how much this means to me. I still have my diploma and it hangs on my wall alongside other accomplishment medals/certificates that I have.

For that, I do have to congratulate myself and even my mother. While the delivery style was not the best – the intention was. So, Thank You Mom…here's a big MUAH!

Now this same determination that got me through my teenage years I also used in helping me leave home. Early on, I promised myself, one way or another when I turned 18 years old, I was moving out and would never go back home. I SERENA CAPRICE DALLAS was going to leave the chaos, the abuse and finally set myself up for something different. I just had no clue what that "different" looked like yet.

In retrospect though, it's remarkable what a person will do to hold on to a promise they make to themselves. Regardless if the promise is consciously made or not. How a person can twist hurt into even more detrimental hurt. How they can have no idea how to live outside of the hurts they know because they are "comfortable" with the limited belief that life really is a choice to be different.

With a huge finger pointed right back to me, I seemed determined to re-live my past albeit with different characters. Worse still, to hear the same phrases that hurt and cut me deep to the core, be uttered by my own lips. Honestly, I thought for sure I knew what to not do. I knew the pain of my past. I should know better.

This is the time that a seed was planted for me to understand that I was the only one in the way of me changing my life. Situations *needed* to happen that would water that seed.

What was the seed?

Learn the lessons of choices, obstacles,

and determination.

Here's where it gets interesting.

Now I am going to get real vulnerable here with you. I believe this has always been one of my biggest challenges. Every day I am aware of that word. Vulnerability. It goes without saying (yet I am writing it) part of my journey is the realization that I am okay with being exposed. Why? It is my hope that you understand that you are still LOVED for WHO YOU ARE. Not for what you did or hope to do. Just you. I am consciously making the connection in my mind that I *can* be vulnerable and be ok; love & accept me. It's OK.

So, at the age of 16, I had four life altering events. The first was to run away from home with a group of other teenagers. The second, commit my first (and only) criminal offense, but boy was it a doozy! The third was to "tell someone" of power about the abuse. Oh, wait there is a fifth one...I discovered my future husband.

Sixteen is such an impressionable age. At that time in my life, other young girls are looking to celebrate their "sweet sixteen" here I was, hiding anything and everything about me. I had learned to close myself off to the world. I was really good at telling stories of how great my life was.

The truth is I learned valuable lessons at sixteen. The first two proved to me that running away can be an answer but breaking the law never is. The third point finally brought be freedom and yet still another prison.

You see, pressing charges against someone as a minor was not handled the same way as current day. I can't believe how archaic the system was back then. Here were my choices and yes, they were limited and ALL MY DECISION.

One, press formal charges against my abuser – my siblings had no clue this was going one. Doing this would mean I would be single handily destroying our family.

Two, broker an agreement to ensure that he had no contact with me should I return back to the home but no one would still know what happened. I guess I failed to mention that when I ran away – this is when I committed the criminal act upon which I was arrested for. During my stay in Juvenile Detention is where I was presented with options as I REFUSED to be remanded back home.

Well, I was incapable of destroying my sister's lives, ripping their father from them. So, after learning that they had never been a target of this abuse, I opted to go back home knowing that he would not be permitted to be near me or alone with me.

Regardless, of course, the internal damage was done. The mind games or mindset; however, you want to call it, was rooted and set. I equated having sex to being loved. I learned rather quickly that when man tosses you aside there is generally another one ready to step in to *"show their love"*. After a fair amount of protected promiscuity (thank goodness I had that sense of mind!); looking for love, validation, and acceptance. There came a day where it all "stopped". I met my future husband at the tender age of 16.

Finally, some peace.... right?

The scene seemed romantic and perfectly laid out. Here I was sixteen (soon turning seventeen), he twenty-one. At the time, it was pure perfection to have someone see me. Truth be told, I saw him, waved at him, and encourage him to come in from across the street. I was working as a ticket girl at a local movie theater. To tell you the truth, I thought he was familiar to me as someone I had previously met, who happened to be hot as well. Well, when he crossed that street, to come check out who was waving at him. I had realized I had no clue who the hell he was. We started chatting, both of us pretending like we knew each other. Man, we chatted for a long time.

That memory is still clear, he gave me a Genesis album. Crazy how it stands out to me as the first time anyone had given me something where I did absolutely nothing to earn it. It was in that moment, I believed I was "in love". By the end of our chatting, we both eventually fessed up that we each had no clue who the other really was and that we did not know each other at all. At the time, it *was* funny, in its charming and quirky way.

This was the basis of our relationship. I saw a hot guy, waved him in off the street, he gave me something with no real intentions. This was our "story". We dated for a short while, then planned our moving in together. By plan I don't even really mean plan, more like, "Hey I need a new place and you want to move out, so yeah". WARNING – this is not word for word – but you get the gist of it.

This started my planning for leaving the nest. As an 18th birthday present to my parents, I moved out. At the time, I thought it was a creative gift. Hindsight, it was cruel to my mother and my siblings. Yet, I believed in my heart that it was exactly what the adults all wanted. My ability to understand, decipher and reason a situation was beyond me. Everything I perceived around me was skewed by my experiences. I just didn't know it at the time. I sincerely believed everyone wanted me gone.

Personally, I needed to be gone. I couldn't live the lie that was in that home any longer. I couldn't laugh, I couldn't dream all I could do was think of death. I needed to breathe again. To somehow find my voice. You see, while no further sexual abuse happened, I never had the opportunity to deal with the effects. I was caught in a quagmire of hate and love of my abuser. I had been secretly binge drinking, was smoking at least a package of cigarettes a day and smoking pot that was easily available in my house on a daily basis. I was in a whole new prison and the only way out was to truly break free of the walls of confinement. Little did I understand that the wall was not a physical wall at all.

My future husband was my "out". At the time did I recognize that I was running from one problem while creating another one. This also meant I had to depend on someone still. Although in my mind with would only ever be for "*short bit*". I justified this as a stepping stone I could use and then get on with the plan of "being something specular"

Reality check...

- I was living with a man, in deeper poverty than what I was living with my parents.
- I committed myself to a person who himself had experienced deep pain and was searching for something to close the hole he had.

Here's the thing, I rationed in my mind that he was a super awesome man who had his own world of hurts. BUT, I could support him to show him I loved him. I would be committed to him and in turn, he would be my "savior". Now here was the kicker. Both of us were looking for salvation; in each other. Neither one of us able to give it. Worse yet, we couldn't *admit* it.

We could not admit that we were broken individually and that we needed to accept that hurt, learn from it, and then grow from it. FIRST.

Needless to say, the marriage did not last.

Broken people can't fix broken people.

No one can fix anyone.

It was not too long after our second child was born that I believe we both realized that we were drifting apart. After each child, just like my mother, I also suffered from post-partum depression; an undiagnosed mental illness which left me either continuing attempting suicide or acting out with extreme highs to extreme lows. Post Traumatic Stress Disorder which had triggers which to this day still haunt me. Of course, we never talked about those things back then. In fact, much of it was chalked up to the fact I was too young and naive.

Around this time is also when I started gaining a lot of weight. I was creating a protective barrier in the hopes of shielding myself from the hurt of the past, the hurt of the present and the thought that there was no future to look forward to. I desperately wanted my husband to make me happy. I was begging and needed him to make me happy. Even though it was never his responsibility to make me happy. I didn't realize it at that time, this was all my choice. Even though I left my siblings and parents, I was still in this self-induced prison. My ability to accurately perceive what was happing around me, in my life was not accurate. Not even a little bit.

While I felt like a failure as a mother, I did attempt to shield the kids from alcohol induced violence. But seriously they still experienced it. Maybe not the extent that I experience, but those verbal tirades that I would go on. They could cut down anyone. They would be minimal, but when I had an outburst is was violent slur that seems to come out of nowhere. Instead of talking out loud how I was feeling, I would "keep my mouth shut" and then swoosh.... release my venomous words. I could see how I was doing to them exactly what I said I never wanted.

The messages must have been so cluttered to the kids. I would speak kindly and hopefully much of the time. Telling & believing that I was sending a message that they can choose to be anything in the world that they set their minds to. There was never physical in the ways that I experienced as a child. Yes, they had punishments but never to break them. Most definitely never any sexual abuse.

But the verbal abuse and the pain I was carrying inside that no one could possibly understand. This hurt them. By them I mean both the kids and my husband and it also hurt my chances of having a successful marriage. I convinced myself that I was at least doing better in one area than my mom.

Reality Check...

The reality is that I failed. We just had different areas that we failed in.

How do you wonder?

- I had 328 heavy pounds of weight on my 5'6" frame.
- I had no value or love for myself much less those who needed me. One cannot give what they do not have.
- I had a long standing undiagnosed manic depression, Post-Traumatic Stress Disorder along with self-loathing.

All this hurt lead me to….What I call….

"My Epic Reality Check".

This came about in my final attempted suicide.

This shit is getting real

I was 32 years old & the year was 2001.

For an entire year, I felt completely void of life. I had never been so broken emotionally and spiritually. No family or friends, no one knew who I was. I didn't know who I was. I felt the most alone when I was surrounded by people.

There are days even still, here in the present when I take a moment to look back I shake my head in disbelief. I cannot fathom how I did this to our children, our family and most importantly to me. I also recognize that I had no capacity to understand what was really going on in my life.

Without that fateful day, I would not be where I am today.

REALITY CHECK....

- That is the day, I made a conscious choice –
  I asked for help.

I was finally motivated enough to say I was sick of living in the past that haunted me. I was tired of holding my mind and body hostage to it each day. How this past had never motivated me, ask to be, or to do, something different.

Yes, I was finally ready to accept responsibility for my actions. Which some of those actions were to end my life. I, Serena Dallas had finally realized that I made a choice. It was a choice to break free from my self-imposed prison. It was the first time I did the following two things.

Accepted responsibility

Acknowledged I chose to live in the past

My husband found me in a medicated overdosed state in the bathroom of our townhouse. I had also used a steak knife to try to cut my body but I was too drugged to make the mind body connection. I was secretly drinking a mickey flask of vodka a day and this fateful day was no exception.

I was so desperate to finally end the pain happening inside of me and the pain I was causing everyone else that when admitted to the hospital and drinking charcoal I will still telling everyone if I leave...I will succeed. I will finally complete something that I started.

Now I look back on that night and I feel a huge sense of sadness for that woman I was. Feeling all alone and believing that death was a better option is a pretty desperate belief system to have. I am horrified at what kind of legacy I would have left for our children. The pain of knowing that they may have felt responsible. Everything I was attempting to resolve with my suicide would have actually **increased** if I was successful. Thank you to the universe for stepping in and having me say out loud to not let me leave that hospital.

Thankfully though, when I was hospitalized, I asked, or more accurately .... demanded and then yes, made the choice to *accept* the help I needed. I had to finally recognize what I had done in my life up to this point. It was not serving me well. It was not serving my family well. It was time to change it all.

While being hospitalized, I welcomed it as a place where it was perfectly safe to yell, scream and tell everyone what they didn't understand. I was ready to stop living a lie. The real me was broken and needed fixing.

Reality Check...

Yes, my childhood was horrific, traumatic, and quite dramatic; there is no denying it. What was even more disastrous though, was my choice to keep living *in* it. That revelation alone was my turning point. Here I was, willingly living in my past. The very thing that I was saying I wanted to break free from each and every day.

I chose to not ask for help....

I chose to not believe that I could live the life I wanted...

I was experiencing this pain still all because of one word...

Choice

The outcomes from 2001 were dramatic for everyone who was a part of my life. Some of those changes were good, others great while still others brought out new pain.

Without a doubt, one of the more painful points was that my marriage ended.

You see, we grew farther apart. The strange reality was, while love was always there; we could not focus on working on a life where both of us were committed to each other in a way that supported each of our needs. I was learning who Serena was, learning what I wanted from myself and from my life partner.

We were no longer the right fit for each other.

I will forever be grateful the relationship we shared. There is still a sadness to some degree that we could not provide each other what we both needed. The sadness that our kids felt the pain of coming from a "broken home". Both of us never wanted that for our children. Both of us were from broken homes; where parents were not capable of co-parenting and raising children together in separate homes.

What I am exceptionally thankful for is that we have made some peace, I believe with each other. We will always share an unspoken bond. We were just two grownups who were kids having kids. I also believe there is a sense of strength that we both realized that we loved each other enough to no longer be with each other. My hope is our children understand staying in an unhealthy relationship is far more damaging than leaving. I am thankful that we both see each other on occasions and we can be kind to each other. He made a choice just as I did. He is true to himself and has created the life he deserved.

An area I feel both of us agree, that our children mean the world to both of us. We both haven't been great parents. We certainly tried to do our best. We didn't do it perfectly but we tried.

Reality Check...

The biggest lesson I learned with the mistakes I made with raising our children. I can clearly **see** the areas where I failed. I can also see **how** I failed. I no longer make up petty excuses as to **why** I failed. Certain things have happened which helped in producing that failure. Although, the ultimate accountability is mine and mine alone.

One day, my hope is that our children will find a way to understand our failures but also realize that they were the most amazing gifts given to our lives. Lessons that are learned are never really failures only those which we decide (chose) to not learn from are.

Here is the kicker to sum up all of this. The first 18 years of my life were filled with circumstances that were mostly *outside* of my control. The second half of my life up this point here was my ***personal choice*** to keep holding myself in the past. I used it by blaming everyone else along with the experiences of my life. Even if it was unconscious, I was still "using it".

Yet, I could have chosen differently. I always had the ultimate power to do so. In choosing to not deal with my hurts, emotions and to ask for what I need, I choose to then continue on and to be the victim.

I had all the power.

At this point as we move on to the next chapter of my life. This new chapter reminds you (and me) that it is never too late to figure out your worth. That you are worth the energy it takes to be you, the authentic you.

Do you remember me sharing that as a young child I was a dreamer, a story teller? Then as a pre-teen how I knew I was going to reach a lot of people and change my world. Those secret passions, they were going to follow me, remind me during my healing period, my life changing period and the realization that they never left.

As you are becoming aware, it is time for a....

Reality Check...

The Story of My Happyness Keeps Growing

"DREAM A LITTLE BIGGER, SET A GOAL AND THEN GO BIGGER"

This last section is all about the choices, the growth and defining real happyness. Yes, here I go again with that whole spelling happiness incorrectly. But my "y" in the word is purposeful and this is my book, my story and it IS meant to stand out because my happiness is chosen every single day.

No matter where you are in your life. Regardless of your circumstances. Regardless of your pain or your victories.

Remember this very powerful statement. Write it on your mirror.

"You **always** have a choice." And not making a choice is still, in fact, a choice.

Remember how I shared about the fact that up until 18, most choices were outside of my power. Most of us are under the direction in some form or another of our parents or an adult.

As adults though, we can choose how we want our lives to be.

That first step is the acknowledgment of the power of, you guessed it.... choice.

Once you have accepted that you have this incredible power. There is virtually nothing that can stop you. Every action is a direct result of your choice. So, as long as you take back your superpower, you can then move on the next part of the equation.

The second part of the equation is to dream. Yes, you read that right. Dream. So many of us have stopped ourselves from experiencing the "what ifs" of our lives. Dreaming is that exciting state where you can picture yourself doing anything you want, regardless of skill, talent or funds. Dreaming allows hope. Dreaming is fundamental to picture yourself as the best version of you. No, it is not foolish. No, it is not wasted energy. Everyone; and yes, I mean everyone, should allow themselves to dream.

Try it.

Don't judge it or dissect it.

What are the first "crazy" thoughts that come to mind?

Whatever that dream is, believe that you can move towards it. What does it feel like? What does it smell like? What does it taste like? What is happening around you?

No seriously go ahead, release your superpower.

You know what I love about dreams? It is that in them are the possibilities of who you really are. In them are unadulterated "don't care if you got no skills" you can dream .... dreams. In those dreams comes the feelings of hope. From hope gives us vision and from vision gives us goals to set upon ourselves to achieve that dream.

I hate to break this to you if you are reading this and you have muttered the words..." yeah but I don't dream". I call bull crap! We all have dreams. I do and so do you. We may have dismissed them for one reason or another but they are there. It is a secret place in our minds or heart. It is a point when you think about that thought and "dream". Then low and behold a small smile creeps onto your face. What happens next for many of us is that when we realize the smile, we disregard it. Purposely shaking it off... because it may be too *silly*.

Can I ask you a question? Have you ever wondered "What if your dreams actually played out in reality? Ask yourself the following.

- Do you get comments from friends/family/co-workers about things you "should" be doing and you find yourself responding with something like, "awe thanks, but I do this because I really want to help, I couldn't really make money at it"?

- How about dismissing ideas because in your mind you just don't have the training or the what the world perceives as "smarts" for it?

REALITY CHECK...

I am here to remind you that I am a living proof, an example right here in this book, for you. Ok, I want to pull the proverbial heartstrings. I had spent far too many years lost in hopelessness. Dreaming was considered silly and improbable to do anything worthwhile. The world needs your light, ***dream it***. The world needs what you have.

Lemme ask you "What would your life look like *if* you were doing XYZ?" (whatever that was you wished you were doing...right now?)

Reality Check...

Chances are right now you are thinking. Serena ...you don't get it. I am super happy that you found a dream but this is just wonky crazy stuff and quite frankly I can't even see how you jumped to this from telling me about your pain of the past.

Your right.

But this is one of those lessons learned in my journey. You see the choices are the superpower that you have no matter what. But trying to figure out who you should be when you have been spending most of your life being what others wanted. That is just not going to "just happen" In fact, first you will have to relax and allow yourself the opportunity to feel who you are. Those "dreams" ARE you. They give you an indication of who you want to be.

Interesting thoughts eh?

Ok, now back to the task at hand.

I am going to ask you to stop right now. Take a deep breath.

Throw away what you feel is the world's perceptions of whatever you need to achieve prior to starting whatever you want to do. (No Ph.D. required; no special skills etc.)

Can you picture yourself in the thick of *Doing* what you dreamed or your purpose?

What does it look like?

How do you feel?

What is different?

Seriously now for real, take a moment to take a deep breath and think of the last four questions. First say your responses it aloud. Allow your brain to hear what you sound like.

DO NOT JUDGE what you are saying. Don't filter it to make it "sound right". Instead, just hear what you are saying.

Did you find yourself at first thinking positive and then when hearing what you said it made you doubt what you dreamed or your perceived purpose?

Here is the power of words. Here is the power of your mind. I absolutely love this long-standing quote from Henry Ford.

"The Man who thinks he can and the man who thinks he can't, are both right."

Which one are you?

The power is all *in* you and clearly, applies to males and females. Speaking as a woman though, I know that sometimes the emotional self can come into play. You may want the dream and believe in it yet you will believe what you are dreaming of or your purpose is "selfish". Its okay ...this is supposed to be selfish. Caring for your self is a good thing! Man, or woman.

Let me also be clear about something very important. I am in no way suggesting that this isn't going to be **work**. Yes, I said the dirty word.... work. Something worth having at first starts with some work. What I am saying though is the power of your choice combined alongside your thoughts and then your words will make all the difference.

They all work together to form the next part.

Mindset

Reality Check...

The only person who has stopped you from experiencing what you want in your life is...

YOU

Yes, I am dropping the proverbial "microphone" bomb here. Please do bear with me now. I say this with tremendous humility. Remember, I was here before. I was the only person who has stopped me from living the life I wanted.

You see, I found comfort in blaming the past. I found comfort in the knowledge that if I didn't try, then I really didn't fail. Strange thing though, all the while I was finding comfort in these things, I was dying inside and I was failing miserably in my own life. So, when I say to you and you read these words,

You alone are responsible for your life and the outcome thus far.

I have read these words over and over again many times over the years. I read them, I have typed them and acknowledge that I have comfortably lived my life and I was miserable. Only when I became uncomfortable, my life changed...dramatically and crazy enough in the way I was dreaming of.

Henry Ford also said another great quote

"Failure is simply an opportunity to begin again, this time more intelligently."

Now, I am not a fan of the word failure, just seems like such a harsh word. But I do regard failure as an opportunity to further succeed; just with more knowledge.

Hopefully, at this point, you have taken the time to stop, breathe and tried to dream. Maybe you even found your dream or a potential purpose. With these next steps, my hope is, it means that you have decided that you going to *allow* yourself to believe that you can *move towards* it.

Here was what I realized in 2008 with a dream.

"My dream was to be an author, entrepreneur & professional speaker. I am going to share my story so you can learn faster than I did."

This seemed like an out to lunch kind of dream. The kind of dream that only people who are really well spoken, well read and in my opinion only the super smart should do. Yet, I can't deny that this is the dream that came to me over and over again. What was even more profound is that whenever I read those two sentences I would get the biggest assed smile on my face and my heart would get giddy. Now I have no idea how to convey "giddy in my heart" but dang; the dream just fit!

This brings me to the logical question is...What's the next step? You need to set up some defined goals that start to get you moving in the right direction.
Have you asked yourself what do you need to do to move towards this dream? Do you need ...

- Resources
- Education

- Support or a mentor

Take a some time to think about it.

I then like to ask this really important question. Take the time to read it carefully. It generally throws everyone off.

"What do you really **need**?"

I find this is where things can get a little tricky. Why? Well, because I am going to ask you to step aside from what you **feel** you need versus what you would really need to achieve this goal? So, if you were like me back then, you probably saying.... "what the heck do I mean?"

What I learned during the process of discovering a dream and then taking literal action towards that dream; is this, "We can get pretty caught up in the planning of what you need instead of moving *towards* the goals needed to make the dream a reality."

Here is my real-life example.

This was honestly my biggest obstacle in my learning. All because I was fixated and then stuck on the technical or logistical facts. I ended up that I did not take any action to, well...move towards the actual goal.

I already eluded to the dream of this book. That dream happened in the early stages of 2004. I convinced myself that I could never really write a book. In school, my teachers always told me my writing was one big long run on sentence. English simply is *not* a strong point for me. My personal perception is that I write like a fourth grader. Sheesh, I know of some fourth graders who write dramatically better than I do.

I then became obsessed with the research portion. Not even on the topic of what I wanted to write about. Instead, I became obsessed with researching the "How to write a book". I made sure to take part in webinars, info sessions chatted with other authors and even with publishers. Each time I did research, I felt even more inadequate about my skills or abilities as a writer. I also created a new fear. What if no one would ever read my story? Would they relate? Probably the biggest fear was "Would I now be ruthlessly taken apart for all the things I kept in secret?" The judgment factors. Oh, did I mentioned that I did all these things yet never once wrote a single word during the "research" to determine if I was even qualified to do this book!

At the end of it all, I finally remembered one important detail. I am a story teller. I can share with you one-to-one some of my challenges in life and use it to inspire you to overcome your personal obstacles. This is what I do when I try to share my story. But I also want to motivate and inspire a world of women to be on fire to their passions. To take that passion and in turn, teach a new generation of women who are leaders and game changes. Yes, I can tell a story with more passion, heart, and emotion. Heck, I will even cry while telling it because I never underestimate what I have achieved since learning of my power. I am a very animated French Irish Leo! Without a doubt, my French background comes out big time when I talk. My way of talking is looking at you and starting a conversation with my story. Not lecturing you about what you're doing wrong.

Writing on the other hand...

As you have clearly read up to this point, my grammar is sub par. I freely admit the next Stephen King I am not! My thought process appears random and I must control myself to not insert those silly yet fun emoticons! I do critique every word written on a page. In the past, I have allowed myself to get stuck on these points. What could have been written in very short time has taken me almost five years from acknowledging the dream and 13 years from the birth of the title of a book!

What changed?

One day not too long ago – okay I will admit just about a year ago.... I took my own advice. I asked myself "what do I *feel* I need versus what I would ***really need*** to achieve this goal". I revisited that dream of being an author. My working title back then was "Hey You, Get Out of the Way". While I had no clue what the title meant or how it was going to look, I just started typing.

I did this with no judgments.

Within a one hour, I had written almost 1000 words. Did I want to analyze it? Damn straight I did. Did I want to correct everything I wrote? Um, yes. But I didn't. I allowed my brain turn off, be in the moment and I started the process of just dumping my thoughts into my fingers and let myself type.

Then I found my next steps. I sought out other writing groups to connect with where we all just got in a room to write. Everyone doing their own thing. I just kept typing.

What was the result?

Quite frankly, it is so simple really; you are reading this.

Seriously, I call this a huge success. Score one for me! This book which may not change the world as we know it. What it will do is change one life at a time, it started with mine, hopefully yours is next.

I made another choice to get over my "*technical*" what I need to start moving towards my goal and started moving towards it. I had made the choice to take action and chose to be open to various opportunities as they presented themselves.

Reality Check...

Are you ready to start setting up some small goals or steps to achieve, so that you are moving towards your dreams?

I have to come clean here and admit something to you. There is a catch or cost to this. The most important catch or cost, is you do have to make it a priority. No, wait, scratch that, I will rephrase that.

Make **<u>YOU</u>** a priority.

You not living your purpose or dream does not do this world any good. Do you realize that there is someone in this world who has been waiting to hear you, see you or be touched by your dream? Each of us has a life purpose. Don't believe the lie that you "think it has no value to anyone."

What you should know though is this. You are literally preventing light from entering someone's life by not living *your own* authentic life.

Yes, believe it. There is someone is waiting for you. Whatever the dream or passion is, they are waiting for *you* to impact *them*. It honestly does not matter what your dream or purpose is.

"That dream or purpose is in you because it is meant to reach someone else. So that they too can reach their own dreams or their purpose."

Every now and then even I surprise myself when letting my thoughts flow. You owe it to yourself and the person who is waiting to share your dream with the world. How is that for an interesting twist!

So, you clearly understand that you need to take actual action to move towards the dream. Remember try not get hung up on details. Don't focus on the how's, instead focus on what is that secret fire burning in your gut.

I did mention how I like to start conversations. I approach this next part very much like a conversation. One that you would have with a friend who was curious about how to get started with their goals. Don't overthink this one. The point here is to finally get it out. I am without a doubt not suggesting that you have a timeline at this point where we have hard facts/dates/times etc. Right now, the focus is simply on writing out the goals or steps to release the dream. I like to mix things up so I will mention, whatever the dream is, see if you can.... DREAM bigger.

Let's get started with a couple of thought provoking questions to ask yourself.

1) What would you do if you knew without a doubt that you would never fail or money was not a concern?

2) What does living your purpose honestly look like to you?

3) If you could give one piece of advice to someone – what would it be?

4) What is the first memory you have of doing something you enjoyed, but then it got squashed? This can be a dormant passion waiting to be revisited.

Reality Check...

Have you been reading this and saying to yourself "Sure Serena, easy for you to say, but you don't know me, you have no idea what I have been through and what I am missing in order to pursue my dreams"

If this thought has crossed your mind. I totally get it. I was right there with you. In fact, there is a certain amount of comfort that comes from this "thinking". Clearly, how can you be expected to be true to yourself, right? I am going to show a little tough love here. This is a mindset trap that pops its ugly head in order to justify how scared you feel and of course to stop you.

- It serves only to hold you back.

- It holds you to past thoughts and past experiences.

- Simply put; and I hope you will stay with me here, it is just an *excuse*.

The message has been clear. Those past experiences no longer define you. They only define you because you are choosing them to define you. What happened yesterday has no bearing on what is happening today. You can't change it. You can't even do anything about tomorrow. It hasn't arrived yet. You have only now. I know now that my past, whether distant or just yesterday no longer define me. Again, part of my vulnerability here is that I do admit that those excuses every now and then pop up. They sure do, but I see them for what they are now.

There is a difference now, those excuses no longer control me. My mindset understands that the past was real, but I also have acknowledged that I have the power. When I realize, this is just mindset that serves nothing good. I see it, and then don't give it no never mind. It no longer defines me. I also know it is now a lie!

Yes, A LIE!

The only time you will ever experience a failure is when you decide you don't want to try. When you don't even attempt to move forward with the power you have to choose, that alone is a failure. Everything else, well those are lessons to learn while improving on the last lesson.

The ironic thing is that on your own journey, you are going to meet someone who is right on the road that you are on now. They will think that there is no other way (just like you are). And your life is what will show them that there is always another way!

See it, smell it, feel it – now do it!

I sincerely hope you are as excited about life as I am. I look back on my life and think how many opportunities I would have missed had I been successful on any of my attempted suicides? I think of the legacy I would have left our children with because of the choices I was making.

Now, the sheer thought of my life thrills and excites me! I still get that silly ass grin on my face at various times throughout the day because I feel the difference. The difference of living my dreams instead of simply existing. The power I have in reaching others touches my soul and I am humbled and filled with gratitude that I am able to do so.

My past experiences are no longer, for nothing. They are not hopeless, pitiful tragedies. Instead, they are examples of how there was always a strong person there.

I am now surrounded by peers and mentors who inspire me to move outside of my comfort zones and remind me to always be on the look out to "See it, Smell it, Feel it and now do it!"

Become comfortable with being uncomfortable. It means you are growing!

Getting up each morning for me is an extreme gift from my creator. I value the knowledge I have that I have the power to create change each and every day. I SEE IT and embrace it.

I also Smell it & Feel It. Uh, wait Serena did you just say, "smell it & feel it?". Sure did! Ok, now is a good time to be clear on the whole smelling thing, right? Fair enough.

I learned this practice, I guess, about three years ago where you close your eyes and future see yourself in a particular area that you would like to excel in or achieve. When you close your eyes to the world, the first thing you are doing is now seeing with your mind. You are no longer limited by your current "visual reality". You are free to imagine whatever you would like to see in that same space.

You can now hone in on what you see around you at that future state of yourself. You should attempt to visualize seeing yourself doing what you wanted to be doing or have achieved the state you wanted. When you are here look around to see what the surroundings look like. This is important because it gives you indications of the things you will recognize on your way to that achievement. Almost like the KPI – Key Performance Indicators that businesses use to help them determine if something is successful or not. Anyways, the point is that when you are this state, I have learned that if you can pay attention to your other senses that are associated with it, this can activate another area of awareness such as the smells and feelings.

An example for me is when I think of myself at an event sharing about my life.

The See it: I am at the glass podium; my notes are neatly on the glass top. My microphone is located just below my neck and on the top button of my shirt. I am wearing a loose-fitting dark blue shirt with slim fit trousers and some kick ass heels that rocks in the same blue as my shirt. The room is dark over the audience yet there is a spot light following me as I walk around the stage area. Close by though, there is a glass of water on a chair.

The Smell it: There is a clean smell in the air, similar to like when the carpets have been freshly cleaned. While seated off in the audience area, to my right is the clear smell of vanilla, makes me think of pancakes for some reason. To my left, old spice. The combination of the smells makes me miss home for a quick moment. Only two more engagements until I am back home with the family. The announcer has just finished reading the introduction of me. I get up and walk over to shake their hand and thank them for such a lovely introduction. But she hugs me instead, her hair has the distinct smell of Aqua Net. Immediately I think to myself no one should light a match and smile because I can't think of the last time I smelled that smell. While standing at the podium I realize I can't really see anyone which is perfect because I am starving and the smells from the podium are coming from the banquet room where the private speakers' area is. I can distinctly smell bacon?

….mmmm…bacon.

The Feel it: The auditorium chairs are nicely padded and recline a bit. But they are god awful as far as fabric. I wonder why anyone would design such comfortable chairs yet, pick vinyl that reminds me of the old car hop days and the booths. Oh well, the announcer is almost done and I can walk my way to the podium. The carpet has a pleasant feel under my heels. They don't make the "click click" sound like wood, instead, there is a slight sound as my foot caresses each step. The presenter has decided to give me hug instead of the traditional handshake. While her hair is sprayed to the nines, her skin is smooth and soft. Hard to believe she is almost 70 years young. Placing my hands on the glass podium feeling its crisp coolness it puts me at immediate ease. I belong here is the only thought in my mind. The warmth of the spotlight is the perfect contrast to my hands. Taking a deep breath, my chest relaxes while a smile radiates my face. My eyes wrinkle because the smile is so passionate. I start with a simple "Thank you".

This is my See it Smell it Feel it. It makes me uncomfortable thinking that this will happen in one form. Yet at the same time, it excites me. I am getting very comfortable with being uncomfortable.

Can you see from the example given what that future state of me looks like, feels like and what I am absorbing all around me? What a wonderful thing to be able to close my eyes; I can actually see me standing right before me. That confident, bold and empowered women, speaking to other women that she admires and respects.

This amazing tactic can be used at will. I use it whenever I start to realize that I am getting in the way of myself again. Remember the title of this book is "Hey You, Get Out of The Way" right!

When I am finding I am losing momentum or for whatever reason my "luck" has changed from "look at the great fortune of opportunities I have" to "I just can't seem to find someone to partner with or the motivation to find the next presentation" I quickly realize I am in my own way again. No such thing as luck. I know you "know" that but do you really "know" it?

It almost seems natural when we tend to look at successful people and say that they have all the right contacts or scenarios that came into play to allow them to achieve the success. They also have a ton of money in the bank and skills coming out of their ying/yang. Yep, I have been there too and yes, I have said those things! I thought those exact same thoughts. Because in reality, only those with money and the right skills can be successful.

Bull crap!

Yea, I said it. Bull…freaken' crap.

Back to the excuses again.

REALITY CHECK...

Learn from me here on this one. Take the time to read this slowly, make notes in the margins or in a notebook and apply your own revelations.

What I do: When I actively remember my dreams and have set out a general plan of attack and start moving *towards* the dream things *seem* to happen with "luck". No luck at all really. I have just opened myself up to the opportunities around me. I have chosen to make myself aware and available.

You have this same power.

- You can choose to realize your power of choice.

- You can choose to listen quietly for your dream (passion).

- You can choose to act on it; moving towards the dream with small goals along the way.

- You can choose to harness the skill of seeing, smelling, feeling it so that you can now be empowered to....

Do It

I'm Human So I Can Change My Mind.

DON'T BE "STUCK"

"My dream was to be an author, entrepreneur & professional speaker. I am going to share my story so you can learn faster than I did."

I feel the need to share this once more for a few reasons. The emphasis is based on the reality that we are humans. While we are not perfect, we most definitely carry the ability to change our minds. We are neither robots nor trees. Robots have someone else performing the programming and do not have the capacity to compute human emotion. (insert Spock joke here!). Also, we are not trees that generally formulate deep seated roots that make them virtually impossible to move to another location/path.

Since the inception of this quote into my life, I have been an entrepreneur at minimum 9 times (at the time of my writing). I have been on the search of the right fit for me as a business owner. Ranging from a bookstore owner, multi-level direct marketing and as a full time entrepreneurial/personal coach. Each of these types of ventures has given me a measure of success. None of them on their own could provide me with a sustainable economic lifestyle. That being said though, I have learned so much from the various types of businesses. I've learned that I absolutely want to be in control of my own time. I want to be in control of where I spend the most focus. I also have learned that if a project or venture does not produce a sense of giddiness in my belly, then I am not taking it on.

The flip side to the above statements though, is if I was "stuck" to just one idea of what an entrepreneur was, I may very well be in the first business I was in, completely unhappy as I was always working and my belly in knots wondering how to find the next sale for the business.

The key point for this is allowing yourself to experience more than one way to do something to bring about the vision of the dream.

These days, my work consists of coaching a maximum of 10 clients in a given year. I also choose them based on the right fit and their determination to see a real change in their lives. I also provide training to businesses, I also put on conferences and workshops locally and nationally that emphasizes women to be empowered. I now write periodically for enjoyment and most recently have enjoyed learning about podcasts to share my thoughts with my listeners.

It all looks so completely different than I had originally thought it would or "should look like". My lesson of don't get stuck on what it "should" be instead, be open to different ways it *could* be. I no longer chase what I feel the opportunity should be. That was a difficult lesson to grasp at times. Especially when I became stuck. I was telling the universe there was only one way to do something. Here is the funny thing, it was supposed to be *my* way.....PERIOD. But as this book started early on trying to make clear. I lived a lie when I thought I was in control of everything in my life. No difference here. I can't control the opportunities. I can only control my responses to them and as such, when I open myself up to get myself "unstuck" new luck or rather opportunities arise and I am feeling giddy as all heck!

So, to go from here to there, I need?

WHAT'S STOPPING YOU (FOR REAL?)

If you are still with me on this journey. I have to express my deepest gratitude. It means the world to me that you would take in my life and hopefully use my lessons as starting points for creating paths to help you get you out of the way. So, you too can start to flourish in your own right. So that you can be a light to the person who is waiting to hear from you.

Previously I touched on understanding what you needed to go from knowing what you want to do – those dreams. To moving forward; towards those dreams. To not get stuck on the perceived needs and then focus on the forward movement of just getting started.

By now though, you may have either realized or wondered if you have some legitimate needs to get you from here to there.

Let's be frank and exceptionally real.

Reality Check...

- No one gets through life on their own.

- We all need help and support.

Even in my own life, my children have helped me to have courage. Graciously teaching me to continue to admit where I fall short yet at the same time; they are the first to remind me how far I have come. Somewhere down the road, my hope is that they too find inner peace with reading this memoir.

Then, of course, is my "bestie", she has stood beside me through thick and thin. She came into my life in my mid-twenties and has seen pretty much most of my adult difficulties. Even with multiple moves across Canada while I was discovering the real me; she has been there. My hope is that she knows how much her love continues to this day means to me. We haven't always seen eye to eye. But my desire is that I too am there for her in the ways she has been there for me.

I am also very fortunate to have a very close relationship with one of my baby sisters. She has challenged me just as much as I have challenged her. Knowing that at any time, she is there to hear my voice, she brings a whole new way for me to be grounded.

Then the miracle, after two failed relationships after my ex-husband. The universe brought to me a man who has chosen to stand beside me. He has been an example to me of what compassion and love without restriction *should* be from a life partner.

There are has been a variety of coaches, discussion groups, friends, mentors, and various other peers that I have had the great fortune to learn from over the years. All because I made the conscious choice to *not* do this journey alone.

So, when I ask you to think about what you really need ~ it is very genuine.

What do you need?

Where can you start to gain new knowledge from so that

you don't lose momentum with your journey?

Hello, life is calling...

CARE TO BE IN IT?

The last chapter is really all about asking you this important question:

Here is where I aim to provide you with some strategies for renewal. All of course tested by myself and the hundreds of people I have had the opportunity to share these tips with.

As you have guessed, it takes a lot of energy to create life. In this case, especially the life you have been dreaming of.

So why wait .... let's get started.

This is LIFE calling.

Care to be a PART of it?

Here is the scene, tell me if it sounds familiar.

After another grueling day, you finally make it home. Starving, no food in sight. You are clearly frustrated. Seriously, you just wish someone, anyone really, would make you something nice for supper. Frig, boxed macaroni n' cheese will do. Just so long as you don't have to actually make it. Yeah well, forget it. It's not going to happen.

So, you say *"Meh, I will pop something in the microwave or wait, better yet I can head over to the local fast food place and grab something there"*.

You get your food and eat it quickly. You are not even sure if it tasted good or not, but you think it's a good choice. Now you can "chill-lax". "Ugh -I need to turn off my brain" ...so the mind conversation starts. Either watch "that show" on TV or maybe, ugh "finish that work project". Crazy isn't how it seems you can't complete these tasks during paid working hours? It so does not help since everyone wants something NOW from you at work! Ok, mind what is the vote? You have voted for the brain waster TV. The argument is that in reality what you really needed to do is turn *off* your mind.

The time flies...and now it is four hours later.

What?

Wait?

Where did the time go?

Well, there were those couple of trips to the kitchen to find something to fix that craving for food that seemed to come on so suddenly. We all know that one cannot ignore the seriously intense sweet/salty that had been gnawing at you a long time before you "finally" gave in!

Then in a flash, you realize something. You are now no further ahead from the time you arrived at home.

"Shiat!" you mutter to yourself. You make a small mental promise to yourself – tomorrow is going to be different.

REALITY CHECK…

Except you know. You just know.

You are so NOT going to be different. Not really.

Truthfully, does any of this sound familiar. Yes, it was very familiar to me personally and even with some of my coaching clients.

This pattern of busy – ness.

No not like actually being busy because you are accomplishing something. Instead...the reality is this is UNPRODUCTIVE BUSY - NESS and it makes us (you and me both) miserable!

In this day and age, when technology is supposedly helping us streamline ourselves. We have somehow perfected the art of being busy at being .... well... busy doing nothing. Do you find yourself just going through the motions of life; instead of actually living *in* it.

The it I am referring to is *our own lives*. We tend to notice these circumstances easier when a major life event happens. You know something like an event where someone gets sick. This could be you, a family member or someone close. Maybe it even happens to someone you admire & respect! Whoever it happens to, there is one thing that happens as a result. It causes you Pause or Stop. To take a step back and realize.

Damn, life is short.

Life carries with it no guarantees with a "next day". There is only this moment.

It is in these life event moments you notice that you have stopped for a second and even found yourself saying "I need to slow down." Stranger still is how the old saying of "Stop and smell the roses" comes quickly to your mind. Only to find that when the effect of whatever the event was is now over, you've been SUCKED back into the monotony of life – all over again.

REALITY CHECK....

- *This is LIFE calling.*
- *Care to be a PART of it?*

We always have options and choices available to us. We can choose can *grab life, squeeze it, love it, be in it* and *live it*. Or do we just continue on with the same old same old? The standard go about the day or days, do what we can by doing our best. Finished each day with our own personal favourite bitch session about the whole rut we are back into.

You know that it is about time to ask another seriously profound question. ***Do you want to LIVE YOUR LIFE or have life live you?***

You still with me? I would venture a guess after reading all that you have, that you prefer to live your life. I also think you may believe that there is just too much to do.

I don't just ask questions here, I do my best to offer simple solutions. Let's look the simplicity of this particular one.

"Break it into parts."

Life can be very overwhelming and yes even busy. By breaking it into parts, you can focus on small bits (or bytes) and actually feel like you are accomplishing something. There is also the fact that one must remember that you shouldn't get stuck on just one single way of doing something. Yes, I have said this before, don't get stuck on one single thing. You may need to try different things in order to make things work for you. My personal experiences have shown me that sometimes things work now and then I need to switch to another way of doing. Even at a time going back to the first way. Seriously it is all about being open; available and willing to do things differently

REALITY CHECK....

This one might hurt to read or say aloud, but I do know for a fact that it must be said.

You must **want** to *want* the change in your life. Saying it just out of sheer frustration is one thing. It's quite another to intentionally say that this; whatever "this" is, must change. It, of course, starts with you.

"You cannot change that

which you do not acknowledge".

Dr. Phil

Let's presume you acknowledge that you truly want to change something. Great, let's get into some meat. Now, let's continue on with three suggestions.

By having these tools in your "toolbox", unbelievably, you will be creating more time in your life. It really is more life in your time.

Everyone who takes these suggestions and begins the process of implementing them; immediately reaps the benefits of enjoying a little bit of life and expand it each time.   Sounds like a bold statement. I just works. These steps have worked for not only me – they have worked with others. It works by moving away obstacles and by creating the awareness of all the opportunities.

Sure, I want you to do all of them. At the very least pick one to start with. Although, I sincerely would like you to try each one.

There is no RIGHT or WRONG .... just do.

Yoda

➤ **Number 1:** Either at the beginning or end of the day (your choice) write THREE things you are grateful for in that day. Know I know this is not a new philosophy. You've "heard" this probably a million times over. What makes this different? I will say this. Starting first with be grateful for yourself is one area that is important to recognize every day. You can't truly be grateful for others until you understand how to be grateful for you and for being a part of this life. This really is a tremendous blessing.

Gratitude goes a LONG LONG WAY.

Here a couple of suggestions to get you started. These were some of mine from when I started:

1. Breathing

2. Being able to work

3. A roof over my head

As time went on.... I grew into:

1. The beautiful evening sky lite up in so many colors

2. I found the perfect parking spot today when I was shopping.

3. I didn't take something personally like I normally do!

The point of this exercise is to recognize the good that each day presents to you. Yes, to YOU. There are always things to be grateful for each day. This is a mind shift. You see we get so busy and turned off, that when negative stuff happens we will acknowledge that first. The shift is in acknowledging how much good there is in every day. By seeing this very real part of our lives, we make even more room for even more GOOD to come into it. It is incredible how this principal happens. Yes, this is the fundamental principle of the Law of Attraction in its simplest form.

So, you start with three things every day. Do this every day for 30 days. Watch how you start to find the good. Watch even how there appears to be more time in your day.

How does that work? You are training your brain to see opportunities, growth...the good in life. Less energy is being focused on the bad, unproductive and the energy suckers around you.

What if you gave someone a gift, and they neglected

to thank you for it. Would you be likely to give

them another? Life is the same way. In order to

attract more of the blessings that life has to offer,

you must truly appreciate what you already have."

Ralph Marston

➤ **Number 2:** CHOOSE to focus 30 minutes on YOU each day. CHOOSE how and when you will do those 30 minutes. Split it up, however, that makes sense to your life. For myself, I split it 15 minutes in the morning and 15 minutes in the evening. There are times when I have given myself more time for me. But I must say 30 minutes' works most every day.

Wait …why 30 minutes? Here is an interesting argument that I hear. Most of us will say we don't have time to devote "that much time" to just ourselves. I say this and want you to remember that I too was one of those people. I found excuse after excuse as to why I couldn't take care of me.

The facts are clear and simple. Thirty minutes in a twenty-four-hour day equals a mere 2.0833 %. I was bullshitting myself over and over again that I could not find and give myself just a small 2.0833% focus on self-care. Once I realized this point. I had little excuses.

I also found that most who tried the 30-minutes goal found it easier to incorporate than say 60 minutes. Although, let's be serious. Even that is less than 5% of a day. When you understand this perspective, it does make it harder to argue against taking a little "me time".

The point with this is to make real changes that are relatively easier to do and yes – MAINTAIN.

Now, what the hell should you do with this 30 minutes' block of time (or two 15-minutes block of time)?

How about?

- Watch a TV program you REALLY want to watch (*then turn it **OFF***)

- Prepare your lunch or dinner for the following day. Something YOU actually want to eat and will look forward to.

- Take a bath

- Read a chapter or two for pleasure or self-improvement (not work)

- Write in a journal

- Go for a walk

- Do an exercise DVD (even if you split it up in two 15-minute work outs!)

- Head to the gym with a friend

- Meet a friend for catch up coffee

- Write a handwritten note or card to someone you've been meaning to reconnect with.

- DO NOTHING (my favorite!). Just sit or lie by yourself – be quiet, be still and just BE.

Do whatever YOU want to do. Make it all YOURS.

Life; and all it has in its busyness can have the other 23

½ hours.

"Self-care is how you

take your power back."

Lalah Delia

➢ **Number 3:** Allow yourself to say NO. This has become the lost art in our busyness. NO. For some reason, we have become accustomed to saying YES when we really mean no. Sure, you may want to do something but have you given time to yourself first? Do you even WANT to do whatever has been presented to you? Contrary to popular belief it is very well fine to say NO, and not feel guilty. Except we have somehow convinced ourselves that we "should" say Yes since they must think we are the only ones to do it. Doesn't matter if it just adds, even more, stress to your everyday life. Doesn't matter that it won't get you further in your career or with your spouse, kids, family …pick any area that is suffering. I want you to be picky. This is YOUR life. You don't have to say yes to everything that comes your way. You don't have to feel guilty either. You can't please and be everywhere without it draining you as well. Especially if you haven't really thought about WHY you are saying yes in the first place. Does it even make sense?

"No is a complete sentence and so often we forget that. When we don't want to do something, we can simply smile and say no. We don't have to explain ourselves, we can just say "No". Early on my journey, I found developing the ability to say no expanded my ability to say yes and really mean it. My early attempts at saying no were often far from graceful but with practice, even my no came from a place of love. Love yourself enough to be able to say yes or no."

Susan Gregg

Learn a way to say no without feeling the guilt. Here is a sample script I have used and provide for you if you find you need to "explain" your No.   *"I appreciate that you thought of me for XYZ, but I must say No to your offer (request). I want to be able to do what I have on my plate right now to my very best. So again, I won't be able to accept."*

I will admit that after using this script a few times, I found that it was exhausting when all I wanted to do is just say NO. Now just like Susan Gregg quote, I say no as a complete sentence. The trick though is after you have spoken; you will need to leave it alone.

- **DO NOT SPEAK**
- **DO NOT JUSTIFY**

Do your best to let them absorb this unexpected information first. This will be hard for you to say and for some who capitalize on you saying yes all the time. This will take a few seconds to get over the initial shock. Granted, let's be real about this. It's not going to work all the time. What it will do is by the simple act of saying NO, you are demonstrating to others (and yourself) that you value YOU. You are letting the asker know, you care about doing your best. You respect yourself and are managing your time wisely.

What happens when you start to value your time? You notice you are PART of life and you are LIVING IN it...instead of just going through the motions. You also become more aware of the greatness of your life. Suddenly there are a lot more roses to smell out there.

When you combine all three suggestions together over a period of 30 days. I will tell you that your life is going to change. No, it's not magic. No, it's not going to be all rainbows and unicorns. What it will be, is a life that you are creating.

Regardless of what your past.

Regardless of your current situation.

Baby, there is a whole life yet to be lived.

Now, here I am 47 years old and I am living the time of my life. It is hard to believe that sixteen years ago, I made a horrible choice to attempt to end my life. All because I held myself hostage to the past that no longer had power over me. I regularly remind myself "had I been successful, I would have missed".

I would have never had the opportunity to have learned what I have. That there is life after tremendous pain. There is beauty all around. There are opportunities galore that I now get to explore each and every day.

I am finally happy ~ with **me**.

I am successful because I am **living** my life.

I am rich because I choose to **share** my journey.

I am at peace because I have learned to love and accept me; **just as I am.**

That first step for me in my early 30's was to be truthful and ask. No, wait, scratch that. Demand that I needed help. I made that abundantly clear to myself and to others. Then I accepted that help. From there, I learned that I am much stronger than I ever gave myself credit for.

I also stopped blaming (either publicly or privately) everyone around me. I have forgiven others that have hurt me. Even if they did not feel they did anything wrong. More importantly, I have forgiven myself for all Susan Gregg the poor choices. Realizing that some moments, I just screw up. That's the thing …they are moments. They are not my life.

Acknowledge, accept, learn and move on.

I hope the story of my journey inspires you to realize that you can live, be and do whatever you desire. Regardless of your past or current situation. Regardless of your talent or lack of talent.

I am not unique in this world. There are many people who have overcome adversity. What I am though is unique and bringing this story to you, right here, right now

Oh, how I crave that each of us lives our own lives. It starts first in realizing YOU have all the power. You have this thing inside of you available to you 24 hours a day, seven days a week. CHOICE. My desire is that after reading all of this; you sense that YOU have the power of choice and no matter what as an adult, no one can take this away from you.

I am in love with my love. I am in love with me. I am perfectly imperfect and every day I am moving towards learning and growing. That is my choice.

My message is waiting to reach the masses; to provide hope that there is more. More for you to experience. More for you to do and more for you to receive.

Thank you for allowing me to share this journey of mine. **I love with all that I am my amazing mother. I love with all that I am my older brother and my two younger sisters.**

I own my life and while there have been huge disappointments in it. There have also been huge successes in it. I am here. I have the ability to love my amazing children each and every day. I get to see the world change by my story. I am finally the …….

World Changer

I dreamt up when I was a child!

NOTES

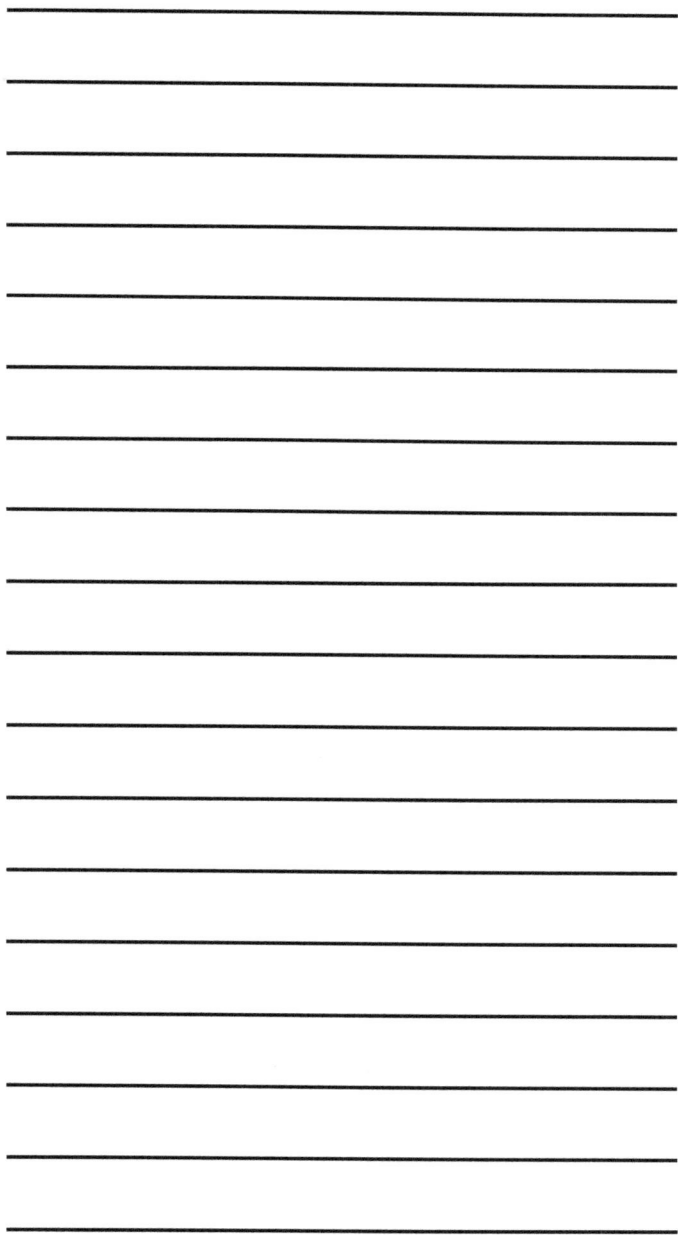

_____

_____

_____

_____

_____

_____

_____

_____

_____

Learn to set your goals AND reach them in the way

that is meaningful to you!

Additional Resources Created by Serena

Setting Clear Goals Series: Tired of setting goals and then they fall flat?

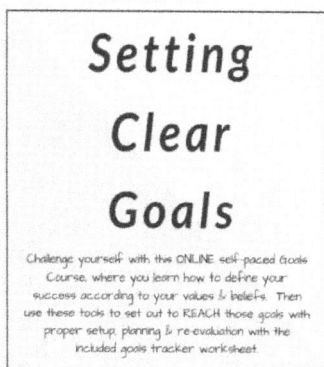

Setting

Clear

Goals

Challenge yourself with this ONLINE self-paced Goals Course, where you learn how to define your success according to your values & beliefs. Then use these tools to set out to REACH those goals with proper setup, planning & re-evaluation with the included goals tracker worksheet.

series

Ready to hear something REAL - IT'S NOT YOUR FAULT.

Goals are awesome when set properly and when they align with who YOU are. Not the other way around.

This is an 8 module online

Time Management Workshop: Personal time management skills are essential for professional success in any workplace. Those able to successfully implement time management strategies are able to control their workload rather than spend each day in a frenzy of activity reacting to crisis after crisis - stress declines and personal productivity soars! These highly effective individuals are able to focus on the tasks with the greatest impact to them and their organization.
The Time Management workshop will cover strategies to help participants learn these crucial strategies.

Visit: https://serenadallas.com/shop for more information

Follow Serena on these various social

media channels for inspiration.

https://www.facebook.com/SpeakerSerenaDallas

https://twitter.com/SpeakerSerena

https://www.instagram.com/speakerserenadallas/

HUFFINGTON POST

Professional Speaking & Seminar Information

www.serenadallas.com

Life Coaching Information

http://serenadallascoaching.weebly.com/